BILLY AND FRIENDS CLASS TRIP TO THE ZOO

BY
DONNA WEBERNICK

BILLY AND FRIENDS CLASS TRIP TO THE ZOO

BY
DONNA WEBERNICK

ALL GRAPHICS ARE TAKEN FROM CANVA AND MADE INTO MY DESIGN

Dear Reader,

Thank you for purchasing my children's book, "Billy and Friends." I truly hope you enjoy reading it as much as I enjoyed writing it.

Sincerely,
DONNA WEBERNICK

Billy and his friends were excited when they arrived for their annual class field trip at the zoo. They were thrilled to be able to spend the day outside of the classroom.

"Children, please exit the bus and form a single-file line while Mr. D. parks the bus," Mrs. Miller instructed.

The children exited the bus and eagerly awaited their visit to the zoo. However, their excitement was quickly hushed by Mrs. Miller, who sternly whispered, "Quiet!"

The first exhibit showcased the lions. Mrs. Miller cautioned the children against feeding or touching them and explained their dietary preferences.

Next, they went to see the giraffes. Mrs. Miller informed the children that giraffes are the tallest mammal in the world. Susie commented on their beauty and size, to which Mrs. Miller agreed.

During a visit to the zoo, a zookeeper approached the group of children to talk about her responsibilities in caring for the bears. She explained that her duties included feeding the bears, cleaning their living area, and ensuring they were healthy. One of the children expressed their excitement but admitted feeling a little nervous about the bears.

Mrs. Miller said, "Let's move on to the next exhibit," which featured monkeys. The monkeys, who enjoyed the attention, delighted and entertained the children.

They performed an impressive
show, leaping from tree to tree,
bouncing up and down, and
creating sounds that made the
children laugh and enjoy
themselves.

While visiting the zoo, the children came across a zookeeper holding an exotic bird and asked if they would like to pet it. Billy eagerly volunteered.

Mrs. Miller suggested visiting the
sea turtles inside the building. The
children enjoyed observing the
turtles swim in their aquarium.

Billy asked Mrs. Miller if they could see the Panda Bears next. Mrs. Miller instructed them to exit the building to get there.

As they were strolling, the group stumbled upon a souvenir shop. Mrs. Miller suggested, "Why don't we go in, and I'll purchase a souvenir for each of you to take home?" The children were thrilled at the prospect of going into the shop, and all responded with gratitude, "Thank you, Mrs. Miller!"

"After visiting the souvenir shop, Mrs. Miller announced, 'Children, it is time for lunch.'"

After finishing their sack lunches, they strolled towards another exhibit, taking in all the sights and smiling, enjoying their day.

The next exhibit the group saw was the American flamingo." Their most distinctive feature is their pink color," Mrs. Miller explained. Lisa remarked, "They are so pretty and pink." Their teacher replied, "Yes, they certainly are, Lisa."

They encountered alligators, and although the girls were frightened, the boys found it amusing. Mrs. Miller reassured them, "Don't worry; they can't get out." The children quickly moved on to another exhibit.

Mrs. Miller suggested
taking a train ride around
the park; everyone agreed
it would be fun.

As they passed by on
the train, they caught a
glimpse of a zebra.

Then, they saw a
zookeeper feeding the
seals and sea lions.

When the children exited
from the train, the teacher
suggested they grab some ice
cream before returning to
the bus.

They were all ecstatic about
getting ice cream. Sally said,
"Thank you, Mrs. Miller, for today."
The other children chimed in,
"Thank you, Mrs. Miller." She
replied, "You all have been well-
behaved today; it has been my
pleasure."

After finishing their ice cream, the children and Mrs. Miller waited outside the zoo gates for Mr. D., their bus driver, to pick them up.

"Here comes Mr. D.,"
Sam said.

All the children got onto their bus, found their seats, and were exhausted from the long day. Mr. D asked, "Did you all have fun?" they all replied, "Yes!" Mark joked, " I need a nap." and everyone laughed. Mrs. Miller chimed in, "That sounds like a great idea." They reached the school after an hour, just in time to head back home.

9 798385 791064